To Grandpa D.M.

Text by Lois Rock
Illustrations copyright © 2002 Diana Mayo
This edition copyright © 2002 Lion Publishing

The moral rights of the author and illustrator
have been asserted

Published by
Lion Publishing plc
Sandy Lane West, Oxford, England
www.lion-publishing.co.uk
ISBN 0 7459 4741 7

First edition 2002
1 3 5 7 9 10 8 6 4 2 0

Acknowledgments
Scripture quotations on pp. 8, 10, 13, 14, 15, 16, 17, 22, 23
and 28 quoted from the Good News Bible published by
The Bible Societies/HarperCollins Publishers Ltd,
UK © American Bible Society 1966, 1971, 1976, 1992,
used with permission.

A catalogue record for this book is available
from the British Library

Typeset in 13/18 GarmdITC Lt BT
Printed and bound in Singapore

The *Easter Story*

Retold by Lois Rock
from the Gospel of Matthew

Illustrated by Diana Mayo

LION
Children's Books

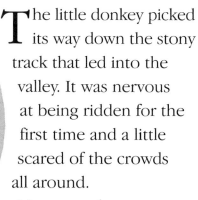

The little donkey picked its way down the stony track that led into the valley. It was nervous at being ridden for the first time and a little scared of the crowds all around.

Many people were making their way to Jerusalem, high on the hill ahead. The Passover festival was coming, and everyone wanted to be at the Temple in Jerusalem for the celebrations.

People began to notice who was riding the donkey. 'It's Jesus from Galilee,' a woman whispered. 'The preacher whom everyone is talking about.'

'You mean the one they say can work miracles,' said another.

'He can. I've seen it happen. He makes blind people see, and crippled people get up and walk.'

Jesus quietly continued his journey, his twelve disciples gathered around him.

The whispering began to spread. 'Healing people is something that the Messiah will be able to do,' someone said grandly, proud of what they knew.

Another added, 'Some people believe Jesus is our people's Messiah. That means he's going to be a king like our great King David of old.'

'That's right,' said a third, 'the king God has promised to send to save us from our enemies – the Romans who rule us and make us pay them taxes.'

He thought for a moment, then shouted aloud, 'Praise to David's Son! God bless him who comes in the name of the Lord!'

Then it seemed that everyone took up the cry. 'Praise God!' they cheered. Suddenly, Jesus was the centre of a great welcome. Some people threw their coats on the path for his donkey to walk on. Others cut branches from the palm trees by the side of the road to make the way smooth.

As Jesus rode through the valley and up the hill to the city gate, there was a joyful uproar.

Jesus went straight to the Temple. In the crowded courtyard that surrounded it, people were buying and selling. There were animals for sale – cattle and sheep and pigeons that could be offered as sacrifices during the festival. Added to the noise of the animals was the arguing and the haggling. Money jingled as people bought the special coins they needed to pay their Temple taxes, and the sellers smiled broadly as they pocketed huge profits.

Jesus watched, his face clouding over with anger. Then, quite deliberately, he went and pushed a stall over, scattering the coins. He turned and spoke aloud, his voice ringing out: 'It is written in the Scriptures that God said, "My Temple will be called a house of prayer." But you are making it a hideout for thieves!'

Then he tipped up another stall and upset a stool. The disturbance frightened the animals, who began to run.

'Get out!' Jesus shouted to the stallholders. 'All of you, get out.' He began to drive them away and refused to let the selling go on.

The chief priests came up to see what was happening.

'What do you think you're doing in our Temple?' they raged. 'And why are you letting people treat you as if you were the Messiah? It's got to stop.'

11

Jesus had no intention of stopping. For the next few days, he and his disciples came right into the city and spoke to the crowds: telling stories and answering all the questions that hecklers threw at him.

'We have a good question,' said some. They were Pharisees – people who had studied the Scriptures very carefully and tried to follow all the laws that

God had given their people. They were sure that Jesus was not wise enough to answer questions about the Law.

'Teacher,' one of them asked Jesus, 'which is the greatest commandment in all of the Law that God has given us?'

Jesus spoke without hesitation: '"Love the Lord your God with all your heart, with all your soul, and with all your mind." This is the greatest and the most important commandment. The second most important commandment is like it: "Love your neighbour as you love yourself."'

Everyone recognized that Jesus was quoting the Scriptures to them. There was nothing in his reply that anyone could say was wrong. His wisdom only served to make them more angry.

The Pharisees and other teachers of the Law talked to the chief priests of their anger, and soon these powerful people were plotting to get rid of Jesus. Then came the chance they needed: one of Jesus' disciples came to visit them secretly. For thirty pieces of silver, Judas Iscariot arranged to let them know where they could come and find Jesus alone.

Jesus knew he was in for trouble, and he warned his disciples. Still, he wanted to share the special Passover meal with them.

He wanted to make this last supper together especially memorable. While they were eating, Jesus took a piece of bread, said a prayer of thanks, broke the bread and gave it to his friends. 'Take and eat,' he said; 'this is my body.'

Then he took a cup of wine, gave thanks to God, and gave it to them. 'Drink it, all of you,' he said; 'this is my blood… poured out for many for the forgiveness of sins.'

Although they did not fully understand, it was something they remembered for ever.

When the meal was over, they sang a hymn and went out of the city. 'You will all leave me tonight,' Jesus warned them sadly.

'I won't,' said the one called Peter boldly.

Jesus replied, 'Before tomorrow you will deny three times that you know me.'

In sombre mood, they made their way across the valley to a quiet olive grove called Gethsemane. There, Jesus went off on his own to pray.

He was fearful and unhappy, for he knew only too well what lay ahead.

'My Father, if it is possible, take this cup of suffering

from me!' he asked God. Then he added, 'Yet not what I want, but what you want.'

Jesus continued praying while his disciples slept. Then, in the darkest night, Judas arrived. He had slipped away, and was returning with a band of armed men sent by the chief priests. 'Arrest the one to whom I give a kiss of greeting,' he whispered.

The rest of the disciples ran off, and Jesus was marched away. The chief priests and the teachers of the Law had gathered in the High Priest's house, ready with lies.

Peter followed at a distance. He sat outside while Jesus faced his accusers and, as time passed and there was no news, Peter felt his courage failing. Then a servant noticed him. 'You were with that Jesus,' she said, 'the one they have on trial inside the house.'

'I was not!' retorted Peter, suddenly very afraid indeed.

Shortly afterwards, another servant saw him and said the same.

'I don't know the man,' he swore.

Then one of the men came out. 'You must be one of Jesus' friends,' he said. 'Your accent shows that you're from Galilee just like him.'

Peter was terrified. 'I do not know the man!' he thundered.

Then the cock crowed as the dawn broke. Peter remembered Jesus' warning, and he went away weeping.

By now, the priests had
made up their minds that
they had all the reasons they
needed in asking for Jesus
to be put to death. Judas,
suddenly sorry, could do
nothing to stop them. Jesus
was marched to the Roman
governor, Pontius Pilate, the one
who had to pass the official sentence of execution.

Pilate was puzzled by the demand. He was used
to violent rebels – people who wanted to overthrow
the Romans and make themselves King of the Jews.
But Jesus wasn't like that. He seemed quiet and
peaceable. So what was Pilate to do?

He decided to please the crowds who had gathered.
It was the custom for him to release a prisoner at

Passover time, and he could ask them to make their choice.

'It could be this Jesus,' he said, 'or Barabbas, whose many crimes are well known to you all.'

The chief priests has done their work well.

'Free Barabbas!' shouted the crowds.

'And Jesus?' asked Pilate.

'Crucify him! Crucify him!' they shouted in a frenzy.

P ilate's soldiers took Jesus. They dressed him in a scarlet robe and made a crown of thorny branches for his head. 'What a fine king you are now,' they mocked. They bowed down to him and sneered, 'Long live the King of the Jews.' Then they spat at him and hit him before giving him back his own clothes and marching him to the hill outside the city.

There, they crucified him, along with two bandits. Above his head they nailed the accusation against him: 'This is Jesus, the King of the Jews.'

People gathered to jeer: 'He trusts in God and claims to be God's Son. Let us see if God wants to save him now.'

Nothing happened except that the sun rose higher.

Then, at noon, the sky went dark.

At three o'clock, Jesus cried out 'My God, my God, why did you abandon me?'

Moments later, he died.

At once, the earth itself trembled and the curtain that screened the innermost and most holy part of the Temple was torn in two. People claimed that strange things were happening – that old tombs were opening and the dead walking. Surely this was no ordinary day.

The soldiers themselves were terrified. 'This man truly was the Son of God,' they whispered.

Several women who had come with Jesus from Galilee to help him in his work came a little closer, weeping as the sun sank low.

A rich man named Joseph from the town of Arimathea came and asked Pilate for the body of Jesus. He took it down and had it taken to a tomb cut in the rock. As two of the women watched, the stone door of the tomb was rolled into place.

The sun was setting, and the sabbath day of rest beginning.

After the sabbath, as
Sunday morning was
dawning, the two women
who had watched Jesus
being buried went to
look at the tomb.
They were Mary
Magdalene and
another Mary.
Suddenly, there was an
earthquake. An angel
came down from heaven
and rolled the stone away
from the door of the tomb.
The guards who had been
ordered to keep watch were
overcome with fear.

Then the angel spoke to the women: 'Do not be afraid. I know you are looking for Jesus, who was crucified. He is not here, he is risen.'

The women ran to tell the rest of Jesus' close friends, terrified and yet full of hope and joy. Suddenly, there before them was Jesus himself.

A great reunion took place in Galilee before Jesus went back to heaven. Jesus' faithful disciples met with him on a hill top. He told them to travel to every part of the world and spread the news.

'Teach people to be my followers, just as you are my followers,' Jesus said. 'Baptize them in the name of the Father, the Son and the Holy Spirit, and teach them to obey everything I have commanded you. And I will be with you always, to the end of the age.'